Jacob w

father of Joseph. He had other sons, but Joseph held a special place in his heart. Jacob made Joseph a beautiful, lavish coat—the famous "coat of many colors."

Next Reader, Please

Jacob's other sons were resentful that Joseph was favored. The brothers' resentment soon turned to jealousy and then hatred.

Next Reader, Please

One day, Joseph told his brothers about a dream that he had. In the dream, Joseph and his brothers were in the fields gathering wheat. Joseph's bundle rose above theirs and their bundles bowed down to his.

Next Reader, Please

By telling this story to his brothers, Joseph was hinting that he would rule over them one day. In their anger, Joseph's brothers stripped Joseph of his beloved coat and shoved him into a pit.

Next Reader, Please

Then, one day, a group of foreigners were traveling through the area on their way to Egypt. Joseph's brothers decided to take Joseph out of the pit and sell him to the foreigners.

Next Reader, Please

After Joseph was gone, his brothers covered his special coat with goat blood and brought it to their father, letting him think that Joseph was killed by a wild animal.

Next Reader, Please

The foreigners sold Joseph to an official who served the Egyptian Pharaoh. The official placed Joseph in charge of his household after seeing that Joseph was protected by God.

Next Reader, Please

The official's wife eventually started pursuing Joseph, but he turned away her advances. Angered by being rejected, the wife told the official that Joseph attempted to seduce her.

Next Reader, Please

The official was furious and had Joseph thrown in prison where he remained for two years. Then the Pharaoh had a very strange dream, so he summoned Joseph from prison to explain it.

Next Reader, Please

Joseph said the dream meant that seven years of plentiful food were coming, followed by seven years of shortage. The Pharaoh was grateful for the explanation and made Joseph second in command.

Next Reader, Please

Because Joseph warned the Pharaoh of the coming shortage, Egypt prepared by storing food for years. When Joseph's prediction came true, people from surrounding countries came to Egypt to buy food.

Next Reader, Please

One day, Joseph's brothers showed up looking for food. Rather than being vengeful, Joseph forgave his brothers and brought his whole family to Egypt, where they were given the finest of everything.

Next Reader, Please

Have you ever been jealous of someone else?

How did you deal with your jealousy?

Next Reader, Please

Have you ever had a dream come true?

If so, what was the dream about?

Next Reader, Please

Although Joseph's brothers sold him as a slave, he forgave them.

Why do you think Joseph did this?

Would most people be so forgiving?

Next Reader, Please

Have you ever had a favorite coat or article of clothing?

What was it like?

Next Reader, Please

Are you familiar with this song?

"I'll See You in My Dreams"

Do you know any other songs about dreams or dreaming?

Next Reader, Please

Thank you for reading and discussing this story!

Would you like to do this again some time?

Please pass your booklet to the leader.